ATHENA TECHNE

Athena Techne

An Assertion of Technical, Civilized Virtue

Lance Miller

Seattle
2010

Contact this.is.lance.miller@gmail.com

Library of Congress Catalogue Number 2010905741
ISBN 1-4528229-4-8
EAN-13 9781452822945

Cataloging-in-Publication Data
Miller, Lance
Athena Techne / Lance Miller
p. cm.
Includes bibliography and index
Library of Congress Catalogue Number 2010905741
ISBN 1-4528229-4-8

1. General philosophy

Cover photo by author of this work: Lance Miller

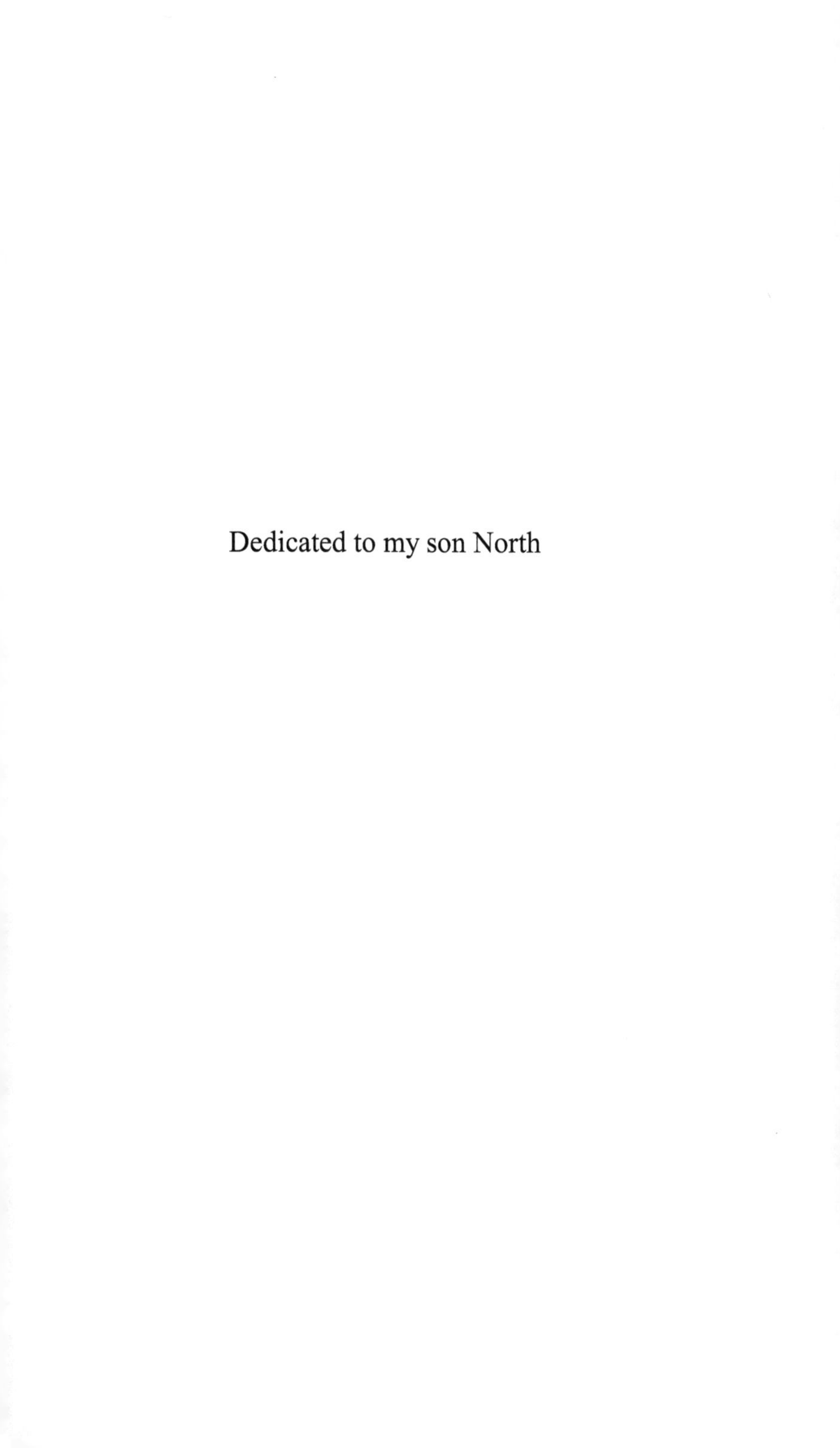

Dedicated to my son North

Contents

Chapter 1
Life and Death at Birth

On January 24, 2008 my wife began her first day on leave from work. She was nine months pregnant, and wanted the last days or weeks of pregnancy to be at home, gathering up her strength and thoughts before the big moment of labor began. A bookish, geeky introvert -she was looking forward to a few days alone reading, journaling, knitting and napping.

This loner's paradise was interrupted around 2 PM that day, when she called me and said her water had broke. We were employees at the same company -a tech company with less than twenty employees, unknown locally, but an Emmy winning technology used by news organizations worldwide. I came downstairs from my hot, loud R&D laboratory and told the CEO and CTO the news. They told me to go, immediately, and someone offered to rush me home.

We live in the inner city, half hour walk from work, and don't need a car. So our drama of the going-into-labor car race to the hospital was different from Hollywood's standard script. We called a taxi. Actually, we packed up our supplies (snacks, clothes, more snacks, and the kitchen sink), went outside, dialed for a taxi from our cell phone, and waited. Patiently. The stories of a rushed affair during this phase of giving birth are pure fiction, statistically. I enjoyed seeing our neighborhood environs in a new light of meaning; standing there waiting with my life partner and knowing we would return with a new life partner.

The taxicab driver was surprised he was driving a woman in early stages of labor to the hospital. He was supportive in every way. He drove at the legal speed limit, and told his stories about childbirth. It was a great way to get to the hospital in this situation.

Upon arrival at the hospital, we were first sent to maternity triage, where they determine whether or not it was a false start, and whether or not to send you home or to a birthing suite. They found there was a rupture of the protective sack around the baby, meaning germs could now travel from the outside world to him. He had to be born before the bad germs caused infection.

Natural processes don't receive orders to do something at a specific point in time, but they can be encouraged to move along. We didn't get sent to a room where a doctor induced labor and out popped a baby. We were instructed our best option was to walk the hallways of the hospital, for about an hour and half, to enlist gravity and working torso muscles to push the baby into a better position for birth.

For me, this was another one of those great moments in our lives together. It was kind of surreal romantic -the quiet, sterilized, well decorated hallways with a view of the city; us holding hands and being very much a couple. We walked around an area of the hospital full of offices and seminar rooms, and it was after 5PM, so almost no one was there. At this stage there was little discomfort for my wife, so the walk was truly enjoyable; a walk that had an added dimension to "recreational". We have photos of us on those walks, and it looks like the most romantic date, the kind of date where the couple only knows about each other.

2 PM, January 25th. My wife had been in labor seventeen hours. The doctors have figured out there is an urgent problem: the umbilical cord is wrapped around our son's neck, and he is slowly choking. Another complication: he is

very large and not fitting through the passageway. My wife and son were both in dire trouble.

At this point I remember the room full of mostly women. Maybe this was a continuum of an ancient pattern, a pattern repeated across the full spectrum of races and cultures. Women clustered around and in charge of baby having. Maybe so, but these women had something more they bought to the room -professional and intellectual empowerment. They had years of hard science and practical, physical experience delivering babies to inform this moment.

We were at the top hospital for having babies in the Northwest section of the United States. Seven hundred babies a month. World-renowned physicians, teams and programs. I'm not writing a promotional brochure, these things matter in the speeding calculus of the moment when your wife and son might live or die. So it mattered, it registered as important, when they said a doctor renowned for her special ability at surgically altering the birth passageway was on her way to the room. When she entered, the entire room gave her a privileged deference. In hindsight I'd say it was because she's smarter than most and gets it done.

The doctors did the surgical work, and told us we only had the next wave of contractions to get the baby out, and if that didn't work we'd have no choice but try a C-section. The waves came in three pushes. My wife pushed so hard on the first push, then the second, when that failed I felt we were up against a wall of last chance. She began the third push. I looked down and saw the baby's head totally outside her body. He was out and on the clean up table shortly. I still recall almost every second of the next fifteen minutes, especially the first time he ever opened an eye, and looked at his mom.

Months after all this my wife and I talked a lot about what happened during North's birth. I came to a realization, and my wife agrees, that if we had done this birth at home, or even been at a less advanced hospital, North would not be alive. Maybe even my wife wouldn't be alive.

At the hospital we had two friends lending their presence and support through a lot of that eighteen hours. They are women with a strong identification with natural childbirth, and "nature is best" in general. I appreciate their friendship, care and support towards my wife. Blunt statement: I am so thankful their values were not in control, I'm so glad our (female) medical science doctors were in control. That childbirth suite had a hierarchy of values, knowledge, wisdom, and practical application far superior, in any respect, to the folkways world of natural childbirth. How can I make such a grand and sweeping assessment of such a complex cross-cultural domain that involves women more than it involves men?

Because my son, and maybe my wife, would be dead -if natural childbirth had been our choice. And in places where natural childbirth is the *only* choice, there are a lot of men who do not hold their child or wife, because they are dead.

Across a lot of time and cultures (from the white Protestant American Old West, to Muslim Turkey, to Confucian China) there are large swaths of family mores where the men are aloof -taking themselves seriously as businessmen, political leaders or warriors; and offering no deep peer connection with their wives and children. We may never figure out all the causes for this kind of society. But I do think I've figured out one cause for men's aloofness and detachment from their mates: the high death rate for mothers and their babies during childbirth. I am not putting up a stopgap to Feminist's perennial critique of these male-dominant societies; I think Feminists are right in their negative appraisal of many societies. But it makes sense on a certain level: to not become too attached to someone very likely to die through the course of what you both will be doing a lot of; having sex and having kids. Lots of wives and lots of attempts at childbirth are a way to leap over the statistical wall of death that faces those without the aid of medical science.

I'm glad I don't face that stark and cruel world without science, where my deepest and most meaningful bonds to my wife and son would not be encouraged. I like being in love with them.

Love
-it's what our modern civilized life affords.

Chapter 2
Skilled Public Workers versus Zombies on TV

If we are going to make our world a better place, or at least avoid unnecessary misery, we need to know how it basically works. There are two opposing camps, serious about improving the world, but who have irreconcilable assumptions of the landscape they both are viewing. One camp thinks we are by default good, and large systemic devices such as government, corporations or organized religions corrupt us. Another camp thinks humans are evil or stupid by default, and large systemic devices such as Judeo-Christian precepts, the US Constitution,

Islam, or the Czar keep us from tearing each other down with exploitation and violence.

These two extreme camps have whole religions, political parties, and college campuses dedicated to promoting their view. Many times in my life I've succumbed to the intoxicating and affirming logic of either camp. I finally started listening to my own life, and my own heart's reaction, and realized these two groups don't have a worldview that explains what's happened around me.

My life has been complex and full of the horrible and beautiful. So has yours. Please allow me to unload an uneven list of the good and the bad -starting with the much more provocative "bad"- that has happened around my one sibling, my parents and me.

The Bad List

1970's. Arkansas.

An eighth grade classmate of mine shows up at school with a gun. He is distraught because his girlfriend broke up with him. The students, who have arrived early and awaiting the bell for school to begin, are assembled outside on the sports practice fields. Our vice-principal confronts the student, and the student says "dance" and shoots at the sidewalk under the principal's feet. The student then steals the office secretary's car and tries to flee to Mexico, and is caught less than two miles away.

The Bad List

1970's. Arkansas.

A good friend of mine, who lives a block away and rides the same school bus as my sister and I, is shot multiple times. He was fifteen years old. He went to the door of an apartment in his same complex, knocked on the door, and an adult inside the apartment opened fire and shot through the door. My friend was hit in the face and chest many times. Amazingly, he survived. I only saw him once afterwards, months after the shooting, and his face was slightly disfigured. He was still prone to smiling and joking.

The Bad List

1980's. Louisiana.

My friend Greg and I are in our late teens, graduated from high school, and working on offshore oilrigs in Louisiana. Greg hitched a ride returning from a few weeks working. They pick up a hitchhiker named Sol. He has a burlap bag. They drop off Greg in Houma Louisiana, and a few miles down the road Sol pulls a rattlesnake from the bag and plunges its fangs into the driver.

The Bad List

1990's. Arkansas

I work the Arkansas School for the Blind. They hire a teacher who becomes somewhat of a friend who comes by our class often to chat. He is normal by all appearances. One day his name is in the news. He had gone to a local mall, where his ex-girlfriend worked, and shot and killed her, then himself.

The Bad List

1990's. McMurdo Station. Antarctica

I was at McMurdo from August 1995 to October 1996. There were two big (in height and weight) guys that were head cooks for the base. They were legend at the bar, drinking an enormous amount of shots every night. They did their jobs well. The roughest time was the winter months, with a smaller station crew and no sun for about six months. We made it through the roughest time, summer sun and new crew had arrived, and the last few days for all of us winter-overs was less strained than the middle of winter.

One of the head cooks suddenly quits working, mere days from completion of contract, and after successfully enduring a year "on the ice". Without his job to go to, he sits in his room drinking and thinking. One day he goes to the housing office and asks to borrow a hammer to pack up his stuff for his flight home. He smiles, and walks with the hammer into the dining hall, and plunges it into one of his best friend's shoulder. He walks back out, smiling, and singing "Mary had a little lamb". He is eventually restrained and kept till authorities come to Antarctica to retrieve him. It is a first for that degree of violence in the history of the continent.

The Bad List

1990's. Alaska.

I'm living in Akutan Alaska, a place with no roads, a village population of eighty-nine, and a fish processing plant that houses one thousand people and takes in a half million pounds of fish per day. It is a strange combination of fast paced at the plant and slow paced in the village. I work at the plant, and friends with many in the village. One day the manager of the Roadhouse bar comes to the plant to buy supplies. When he exits the plant's main building, someone hits him multiple times in the head with a wooden board. I am one of the first to run outside and see him laying and bleeding. I hold him as we drive to the village clinic, he passes out, and I think he's dead. He comes back awake at the clinic. Four months later I see him and all is healed.

The Bad List

2000's. Arkansas.

My parent's, retired, living in the same place that I grew up, are at home watching television. At around 7:30 PM two black men kick in the front door, have guns, and tell my mom and dad to get on the floor. My aunt, who has dementia, is in a bedroom. They find her, too. My dad pleads with them to just take all their money and anything else they want, just let them live. The two men steal some cash and other things, and flee in my mom's car. My mom and dad call me days afterwards, from my sister's home in a nearby town. They never spend another night in their house, sell it, and move sixty miles away. My mom said she heard many times young blacks talking loudly in the street about getting rid of the last few remaining whites in the neighborhood.

The Bad List

2000's. Arkansas.

My sister is walking from a shopping center checkout to their car in the parking lot. A few feet from my sister a man is trying stop a crime. The man, a father in his 40's with his family out shopping, tries to stop a nineteen-year-old black man who is pistol-whipping an elderly white woman who resisted giving him her purse. My sister's eyes are on the 40-year-old father when the teenager shoots him in the head, killing him. The teen flees in an accomplice’s getaway car, and is apprehended days later.

The Good List

1980's. New Orleans Louisiana.

I'm the night janitor at a restaurant, doing complete clean ups while it is closed from midnight to six. New Orleans has lost its initial fun and adventure, and now I'm mostly isolated and barely getting by. I complicated things by being in a small religious sect with no same-age members in the city. On Christmas Eve I'm home alone, reading and listening to Tulane's student run radio station. A waitress who worked at the restaurant knocks at my door, and invites me to her family's Christmas Eve. She is dating the assistant manager of the restaurant, a friend of mine, and he is at her apartment along with her son. We have a great time.

I've never been so alone or disliking my life, this invitation may have saved my life.

The Good List

1980's. Arkansas.

I moved back to Arkansas from New Orleans. With pennies. I move into a bizarre situation -a very large Victorian era home, in disrepair and not legal for renting. The owner allows me to live there in exchange for guarding it. The neighborhood is extremely dangerous. One night someone enters the house, while I am in bed and my room door is locked. I stay still, they walk around and eventually leave without finding me.

My friend Greg comes over one day. He's amazed at how bad my living arrangement is. He offers to load up my stuff and I start living at his apartment. I move, and we begin years of renting awesome places and throwing parties that remained locally famous for years.

The Good List.

Hitchhiking. 2400 miles. USA Western States.

[What follows is a continuation of the Good List, but every story is part of an epic month long hitchhiking adventure on the summer of 1994 with a friend, Beth Shalom. The experience deserves its own book, and it would mostly be stories of strangers opening their cars, homes and lives to us.]

1990's. Utah.

A couple picks us up in Kanab Utah, takes us with them on their day vacation in Zion National Park. We ride in the back their truck on a futon, getting a better view of the mountains than anyone.

The Good List.

Hitchhiking. 2400 miles. USA Western States.

1990's. Nebraska.

We hitchhike to the Winnebago Tribal Pow-Wow. We are fed and paid to babysit Navajo babies.

The Good List.

Hitchhiking. 2400 miles. USA Western States.

1990's. Nebraska.

In Hooper Nebraska there is an old, redbrick bar in the middle of town. The bar owner gave us free beer and let us stay after closing while he cleaned up and played the Who's *Won't Get Fooled Again* really loud.

The Good List.

Hitchhiking. 2400 miles. USA Western States.

1990's. Nebraska/Wyoming/Idaho/Nevada/California.

Freddy, a tourist from Frankfurt Germany picks us up in Nebraska, takes us on his vacation to Yellowstone National Park, then on to San Francisco, where he dropped us off at the corner of Haight and Ashbury. Along the way we stay in a Cody Wyoming hotel, car camp overnight in Yellowstone, and learn to speak a little German. Freddy and I have this instant good rapport, joking nonstop. Looking back, I'm surprised two from different cultures could have such a mind meld.

The Good List.

Hitchhiking. 2400 miles. USA Western States.

1990's. California.

In Bakersfield, California we are invited into a single father's home, and given access to kitchen, washer & dryer, and a room to sleep in.

The Good List.

Hitchhiking. 2400 miles. USA Western States.

1990's. California.

A young computer graphics hacker gives us a ride, and when he finds out we've never seen Carmel California, he goes out of his way to show us the town. We go through the town, stop at the golf course, and walk along the rocky Pacific shore.

The Good List.

Hitchhiking. 2400 miles. USA Western States.

1990's. California.

A football player for the LA Raiders gives us a ride. Along the way he tells us about his football career and being part of Dr. Dre's bodyguard entourage. We stop along the way and he buys us soft ice cream cones and bottled water.

Alright, that's the conclusion of my Good and Bad lists. I know as far as writing goes it was all over the place, the opposite of a tidy or pretty story line.

Paradoxically, tidy and predictable narratives are what get us into trouble. Reality is asymmetrical, it doesn't have to "balance out" or resolve like our checkbooks and movie plots need to. This disjoint between tidy stories and reality is truly a problem in one regard: one of our expectations with language is its ability to help us predict and prepare for the future. (That last statement was a meta statement: We expect language to help us construct what to expect.)

Enough kicking around about meta levels and language theory, I'd like to get back to the "humans are either inherently good or bad" thread. I've been deeply embedded in both camps, and saw the harm both cause.

When I was younger I belonged to a Protestant religion that believed deeply in original sin, and even came up with a catchphrase "Adamic condemnation". That catchphrase is all you need to hear to correctly anticipate the beliefs behind it. Humans did something very bad in the very beginning, in the Garden of Eden. That single act of rule breaking defined us, giving all humans a limit -always being dirty rotten creatures. Of course this same religion has a single lone character that burst past that limit, and wasn't a dirty rotten creature, and to be "saved" we (the dirty rottens) need to join his club by going through certain rituals.

This religion was very intelligent. Seriously. They thought things through. If humans are always dirty rotten creatures, then political solutions are always evil, because they are the work of humans. So my religion didn't vote, because voting "showed a faith in human designed solutions". Since the United Nations is the most grandiose political institution, this religion published many articles portraying the UN as a heinous crime against God. I recall when the UN declared "The International Year of Peace" my religion spiraled into high alert that we couldn't allow such a peace to happen, because peace created by humans, rather than by God, was inherently wrong. We had to, or more like God had to, stop the realization of this secularized peace. A human becoming better via their own design was forbidden.

Progressives often cite Protestants, especially the wacky schisms of east and southeastern USA, as bad examples, but Islam and Buddhism deserve some heat also.

Islam, wow, where should I start? Crime, cruelty and inequality seem to run much more efficiently with a brain, or nation, controlled by "total submission". Serving Allah covers a multitude of sins, allowing converts a wide berth of activity, while all others are heinous criminals (reformable through conversion) no matter how dedicated to good actions they are.

Myself being a typical urban west coast progressive, had to consider attending a Buddhist church. After looking into a local church, I read some of their beliefs online. I've known for a long time "desire" is the ultimate sin of this religion, but was surprised at the degree this church talked about our sin incarnate. I felt this Buddhist church was an entry point for a slippery slope to my old Protestant religion.

Much later in life I completed my Bachelor of Science at a west coast college famous for its extreme left culture. In every on or off campus political forum I attended, the students held a unified theory that corporations, police and the military were the root of all evil. These institutions caused all wrongs, and if swept away, we would be free and good again.

In these social circles I never heard a single mention of the lone insane gunman or serial killer. Several times in my life a lone individual had done a tremendous act of violence, and my college town friends never once allowed a worldview discussion of this. These college friends obeyed a mental or language rule to never acknowledge a perennial part of the human condition. The language game they played led to the inverse of "original sin" religious convictions, these college friends believed individuals can never of their own volition commit horrendous acts or be a threat to society.

Enter Athena Techne, an ancient storyline that anticipates more of our lives than our own dominant contemporary discourse.

The power is not always in her story, but in the juxtaposition of other characters to her. Ares (called Mars in Rome), was her brother. He was a patron of technology, just as Athena. He was a patron of war, just as Athena. The difference begins with Ares enjoying killing as many people as possible (his sons were serial killers), whereas Athena would choose a peaceful course of action first. Ares was dumb as a rock, and lost fights even with mortals. Athena, by contrast, embodied wisdom.

Athena is *techne* ("art", "skill"), rather than *nous* ("mind"). *Nous* is an opposite of sense perception, a purely mental operation that does not mix with the physical world. *Nous* is a perfect and unchanging construct, a "divine" mind.

I know who is controlled by an unchanging mentality: The groups whose fundamental beliefs that humans are by default good or evil. No matter what reality reports back (especially the exceptions that disprove their worldview), they continue with the same mental constructs unabated. They are unstoppable, self-righteous zombies, powered by mind (by nous uninformed by sense perception, a substrate of techne).

I am not picking on God here. The zombies are not powered by God. They are powered by an unchanging thought they got lodged in their head. How do we combat being converted to zombies? By doing what zombies don't do: by being detail oriented, and investing ourselves in those details. Become a skillful public worker, become a demiurge.

The word *demiurge* is a Latinized form of Greek *demiourgos*, literally "public worker", and which was originally a common noun meaning "craftsman" or "artisan". Later *demiurge* took on more religious meaning related to forming and reshaping our world. Although a fashioner, the demiurge is not quite the creator figure in the familiar monistic sense; both the demiurge itself and the material from which the demiurge fashions the universe are the product of some other force.

Today our media are filled with the acts of zombies. By contrast, skilled public workers - accountants, computer programmers, traffic engineers and registered nurses; these manifestations of Athena Techne contain too many details in their daily lives to fit on the big screen. The demiurge weaken themselves with every watching of Zombies on TV; because the time spent detracts from mastery of skill and details, and also allows whatever unchanging idea in the (evil) zombie's head to possibly seep into the (heroic) public worker's head.

Techne can be translated "human endeavor", and zombies are those who have ceased to contribute to human endeavor. Athena Techne is a patron of human endeavor, whereas Ares, her brother, is a patron of bloodlust and dumb violence on a massive scale. Zombies listen to an unending message lodged in their head: such as the Earth Liberation Front message to destroy civilization in order to save Nature, or the Reagan message to downsize government and the public sphere to a point of no use, or Osama bin Laden's call for Jihad. Zombies eventually aggregate together and fight on the side of Ares.

It's always Ares and his Zombies against Athena and her Public Workers.

Techne is *human endeavor*, whether it is highway construction or amending the Constitution of the United States. All techne (technology) needs maintenance. Any society, as a technological object, should not be seen as inherently running well forever without intervention, nor totally run through and through with evil or stupidity. We should expect some degree of upkeep and modification. The demiurge is human endeavor's only savior, and the demiurge is you.

Chapter 3 Straight Lines through Arkansas

Joe: There are no straight lines in nature.

Jane: So the shortest distance between two points doesn't exist?

Obviously we can find the shortest distance between two points. A by-product of that is a straight edge, and with a straight edge we can create the machinery that fabricates other machinery. The human-made world emerges.

When I was five, our family living at 1619 Broadway Street in Little Rock Arkansas, the human-made world leapt into my consciousness. It was such an amazing time and place to have been a small child. We lived on Broadway from 1964 to 1968, right downtown, two blocks from the Governor's Mansion. Blacks were now by law equal, and the Beatles and Rolling Stones had a stronger and more intoxicating message than our old preacher's and politicians. I'm not pulling a Hemingway here (he would instill way too much intellect into small child characters); the issue of equal rights for blacks and the meaning of the British Invasion were very much in my face and in my head in those years.

At four or five I was obsessed with the idea of the straight line and manufactured objects. My main question was how does the lowest-order tool (the tool that makes higher-order tools) get a precise straight edge? All the other objects that are made by it are going to inherit the lowest-order tool's precision. If it has defects, then the subsequent manufactured objects will also.

Our house on Broadway had a small front lawn, with several spots of dirt instead of grass. This was a perfect area to practice my first engineering. I loved cars, real ones and toy ones. I set out to build concrete streets for my toy ones. I chiseled the mortar out of the brick walls on the north side of our house, mixed that with water, and paved little concrete streets on our front lawn.

When inside the house music was always playing, on either the radio or records. We had The Beatles first album, with the iconic and stark black and white photo of the band's faces. My equal favorite was the Rolling Stones *Big*

Hits, High Tide and Green Grass. The Stones album had several pages of photos, really large photos since they were in an album sleeve. I looked at those photos a lot. Those guys didn't look like anyone I'd seen in Little Rock. I kept asking my mom about that -why do these guys have long hair? My mom: because they are hippies. What's a hippy? Hippies don't like war, like black people, take drugs, and are good at music. I decided right then and there hippies are cooler than anyone else.

One subject being talked about a lot, by the adults in my life and on the news, was about blacks. With civil rights legislation of 1964 Southern society was becoming desegregated very fast. The adults all around me were white, and they were constantly chattering about this. I know for the reader it'd be easier to describe someone as a social-justice dedicated 1960's hippy, or a KKK sympathizing white. My family was so far from both these extremes. I think a lot of whites in the South were also. In those years my dad would point to a black family that lived across the street from my great grandmother, and brag at length on how great they were (they were very middle class, immaculate house and lawn, nice family car).

With all this chatter about blacks there were words being thrown around about how dangerous they were now that blacks could go anywhere that whites could. Looking back I don't think it was my mom and dad that put that forward, it might have been the older people in my dad's family. All I can be sure of is I got it in my head blacks were a danger.

During all this, one night I had a -dream still vivid decades later. It was late in the day, and I was on the sidewalk near the Governor's mansion, two blocks from home. I was talking to my uncle Lester, and then said bye because it was getting late and I'd better get home before dark. As I was walking home a black man follows me. Next door to us lived a retired couple, the Reaves. I ran up on their front porch and knocked asking for help. The black man runs up on the porch and attacks me, and I struggle to get his hands. By now it's more night than daylight. He stabs me to death.

About a year after this dream I started school. Not just any school. President Johnson's welfare initiatives included Head Start, a program that provided "comprehensive education, health, nutrition, and parent involvement services to low-income children and their families". I was poor, so I was in Head Start on its second year of existence.

I remember doing a lot of art projects in Head Start, especially making a collage of a frog I thought was a real challenge, listening to a teacher play an upright piano, and one more thing. Head Start was a new welfare state instrument, and this was the 1960's. So who would be involved in such an affair? Radicals. I put all this together years later in my forties. I had one thing I remembered from those classes that never made sense till my adult mind connected the dots to radicals: the women wore no underwear. And they didn't wear make-up. My first year of school was in Radical-ville!

Returning to the fear of blacks thread. Something interesting happened. Or maybe I should say nothing happened, which was a good thing. In first grade I recall an equal amount of black kids to white kids, and I had a black teacher, Mrs. Marshall. She was so classy and pretty, and a great teacher. I rarely got in trouble in all my days in school, but I caused quite a fuss one day in first grade. We watched a film, old style reel shown on a projector screen, and the lights were down. I got caught kissing the girls on my left and right. They were kissing me a lot. One was white and the other was black.

It's no small irony that a desegregated schoolroom was the antidote of prejudice or fear that was sparked by desegregation. I really loved that Victorian era public school, and our neighborhood of old homes, the Governor's Mansion, and the big city park, which was the childhood home of General Douglas MacArthur. But the place we lived in was old and falling apart. Parts of the ceiling were beginning to randomly fall to the floor. We had to move out, and we did, to a nice new apartment in the suburbs of southwest Little Rock.

In 7th through 12th grade I was bussed far out of town. The junior high was in Sweet Home, historically a rural black community. This was through the mid to late 70's, and relations between whites and blacks were beginning to be something different from the 60's. In my own life it was a mix. On the negative side, there was a set of black boys that stole my lunch money every day, and I got noticeably skinnier and unhealthy because of this. On the opposite side of race stories, my best friends were Michael, Alphonso, and Helaine, and also happened to be black. I always sat next to Helaine, maybe the only geek/nerd in the school besides me. I'd say the meanest kids in the school, towards me, were these sort of overweight white boys from my own suburbs, who caused much more psychological harm than the missed lunches.

I lived the next few decades as a middle of the road, nothing special, progressive. Then I paid $50,000 to an institution in the pursuit of a masters degree, and found out about the war on (Platonic) straight lines, civilization, and Athena Techne.

I had sensed such a war since joining the

ranks of the counterculture in my early 20's, and this awareness became more pronounced once I moved to the Northwest, then again more intense when I lived in Olympia getting my Bachelor of Science at Evergreen State College. The Whole Systems Design graduate program at Antioch University was exceptional, a turning point for me. It is there I finally figured out it was a war. Unaware it was war till it was too late, I lost the battle.

Dear Reader, please know my use of "battle" and "war" is not the tired old trope of a rank-and-file conservative enrolling in a liberal institution, hears some lectures strongly slanted towards belief in evolution, gay rights or global warming, then goes on conservative friendly media channels to screech about being offended and their conservative viewpoint being marginalized. I wanted to attend an institution slanted towards belief in evolution, gay rights or global warming.

Don't get distracted by the time and place of my battle in this war, don't get overly focused on the significance of the particular school and program. The war is going on all over the place, it is a world war, and a perennial war. My grad program was just an instance. This grad program at Antioch actually provided a service in the end, by their seeing the implications of Anti-Athenian threads running through the countercultural movement and creating pedagogy with a unified, coherent epistemology and application.

For a guy who lost a major battle in a war, I'm doing alright this morning. I'm typing on a nice computer, living in one of the better neighborhoods of one of the better cities in the US, married to a beautiful woman 13 years younger than me and I get to play all day with my two year old son. But what about those black kids that stole my lunch money, and the blacks that wanted my mom and dad out of the neighborhood (which was accomplished when they were threatened at gunpoint in a home invasion)? Why did they take my lunch money, and why did two black men break in my mom and dad's home and point guns at them? Because these blacks (and their victims in crime) are casualties in the war on Athenian values.

The ancient Greeks deserve some of the blame here. They generated an enduring basis for engineering within their mathematical theoretics, unfortunately these theoretics had religious overtones. Plato believed we don't just count things, such as cows or pencils, with numbers, but that numbers have an existence all their own. Numbers, as Platonic Forms, preexist and are discovered by the minds of intelligent beings. Numbers are more pure than counting cows or pencils, according to Plato and his followers, a kind of pure that is better for minds to contemplate. Cowboys count cattle and get their hands dirty, opposite of mathematicians who stay in their ivory tower contemplating numbers while avoiding the dirt out on the farm.

Mathematicians avoiding getting dirt on their hands are not the real story here. Rather, it is a tendency throughout history for a class to exploit this distinction between mental workers and physical workers. "Mental workers" are most often doing the world a service. But a parasite lurks alongside mental workers. They are "mental" without the work.

Plato set this all up with his pure Platonic Forms and the allegory of the cave suggesting access to the Forms (minus physicality) was access to a greater truth. Throughout Plato's great contributions to the world he committed no crime, he only left the chicken coop door open. Theft of a free lunch came from subsequent generations exploiting the situation.

The Neoplatonists of the 3rd Century AD pulled the crime off, and provided the reasoning and archetypes for subsequent generations. They divorced Idealism from Athena Techne. Neoplatonists made Idealism alone and true, whereas when living with Athena Techne there was a bond grounded in sensuality, and thus, a little less than heavenly.

The Roman Neoplatonists achieved this divorce, basing their philosophy on earlier works of Greeks. But if we review those earlier works of Plato and Aristotle we see a reverence for the marriage of Idealism and Athena Techne.

"*Every cause for a thing passing from not being to being is poiesis, so that manufacturing activities in all branches of industry are forms of poiesis and all artisans and craftsmen are poietai (poets).*"

-The Republic

Techne is "*a capacity to do or make something with a correct understanding of the principle involved.*"

-Aristotle

With Plato and Aristotle we see a respectful status for manufacturers, for "Makers". With Neoplatonism we see the Unmaking of Makers. For Neoplatonists, things that change are inferior to things that do not change. Every iteration of an idea or form becomes less whole and less perfect. I cannot think of a worse mental construct in which to master the human-made world. In technology, few things begin perfect, and iteration is fundamental for improvement.

(Keep in mind this book always means the widest definition of technology and techne: all human-made things including language, writing, government, artistic objects, bicycles, programming languages and electronic devices.)

For well over a millennia Christianized Europe fell into the appropriately labeled "Dark Ages". Major innovations in math and science still occurred in Arabian regions and China, but it wasn't till Modernity that Techne began to expand exponentially, taking humans all the way to the exploration of space and laypeople's use of a global interconnected computer system.

Modernity has been a context for the steady expansion of Techne, the expansion of the manufactured. Along the way, Modernity, while providing progress in the form of universal suffrage and higher living standards for previously enslaved or peasant class people, also introduced manufactured risk.

Before modernity, humans mostly dealt with natural disasters and disease as the bad things of life. Risk was a contemplation of natural forces, and most humans prayed to their God to avert disaster. But with Modernity came manufactured risk, things caused by human agency, such as world wars empowered with mobility of airplanes and tracked vehicles, and factories pumping out bombs that could be delivered and detonated anywhere on the planet.

One of the most popular "manufactured risk" narratives to study, or base one's academic career on, is World War II. That war has everything, including the worst atrocities (concentration camps, atom bombs) and the greatest inventions (computers, jets) known in pop culture.

The New Left movement, which began in the 1960's, and Postmodernism, which began in the 1970's, are what I want to call "The Great Reaction" to the manufactured risks endured in World War II. Whereas the U.N. was a modern, rational, and technical approach to trying to avert a repeat of World War II atrocities; the New Left and Postmodernism appealed more to emotions and an irrational, holistic response to the WW II atrocity narrative.

The New Left (now over forty years old) has been summed up as anti-Western nihilism. I once enjoyed the New Left, it allowed me a pretense to adore Chinese and Japanese culture while living in WASP dominant Arkansas. An experience signaled to me an end to my romance with the New Left. I was standing at the main bus stop in front of The Evergreen State College, talking to a student who seemed to know a lot about Japan and China. He had just completed a lengthy stay in China. I was dismayed when he said he had spent all his time in cities along the western border that had little or no electricity. I felt one had to be under some kind of spell, or obeying some strange ideological directive, to go to China and somehow avoid the most colossal industrial phenomenon on Earth. All through my life I had wanted to squirm out from underneath the assumption that western Judeo-Christian heritage was the greatest, and the original open-ended and exploratory spirit of the counterculture was an appropriate ticket out of town. But with this student's ideological slavery -his going to China and avoiding contemporary industrial China in order to prop up a bizarre Western idealization of Oriental backwardness- I could sense a trap in the now ossified New Left as threatening to my growth and adaptability as was WASP dominant Arkansas.

During the same year, and with another student at Evergreen, I had an experience that forever tainted my view of Postmodern theory. A student handed me a photocopy of her assigned reading, a subsection titled Pyrotechnics within The Lyotard Reader by Jean-Francois Lyotard (Blackwell Publishers, 1989). Lyotard gives as examples a person striking a match for a purpose, and a toddler striking a match for no purpose. Lyotard admits the toddler's actions are destructive, but on the whole, the purposeless action is given a higher praise. The toddler's act of striking a match is "revolutionary", a great thing to counteract the negative effects of functionalism and skill which enables "the Establishment". Lyotard is borrowing and extending an earlier writing, Aesthetic Theory by Theodor W. Adorno, Robert Hullot-Kentor (University of Minnesota Press, 1998), in which Adorno regards purposeless pyrotechnics (fireworks) as amongst the greatest examples of art.

> [Art is] *irresistible precisely because it refuses to let itself be nailed down either as an entity or as a universal concept. Its ether is bound up with particularization; it epitomizes the unsubsumable and as such challenges the prevailing principle of reality: that of exchangeability. What appears is not interchangeable because it does not remain a dull particular for which other particulars could be substituted, nor is it an empty universal that equates everything specific that it comprehends by abstracting the common characteristics. If in empirical reality everything has become fungible, art holds up to the world of everything-for-something-else images of what it itself would be if it were emancipated from the schemata of imposed identification. Yet art plays over into ideology in that, as the image of what is beyond exchange, it suggests that not*

> *everything in the world is exchangeable. On behalf of what cannot be exchanged, art must through its form bring the exchangeable to critical self-consciousness. The telos of artworks is a language whose words are not imprisoned by a prestabilized universality.*

Adorno, and his fanboy Lyotard, posit an ideology in which (to use the most hideous New Age quote I ever heard) "it's all just energy", and those who name things, categorize, build up, repair subcomponents, and iteratively improve are worthy of nebulous, ambiguous critique and opposition.

Remember my ending of the last chapter: Techne is "human endeavor", whether it is highway construction or amending the Constitution of the United States. All techne (technology) needs maintenance. Any society, as a technological object, should not be seen as inherently running well forever without intervention, nor totally run through and through with evil or stupidity. We should expect some degree of upkeep and modification. The demiurge is human endeavor's only savior, and the demiurge is you. Lyotard, and his armies of flame throwing toddlers, are going straight for the root cause of manufactured risk, of the atrocities of WW II (which the French are perpetually freaked out about since they performed so poorly in the contest), and in the process cutting off the root of all human greatness: functionalism, intention, and skill. I cannot think of a worse agenda, a more debilitating and misery-causing paradigm. The word "stupid" is, well, stupid, and not to be overused, or maybe ever used, in proper literary circles. But Lyotard and Adorno's aesthetic/ideological stance sort of begs humans to plumb to some depth of stupidity with a call to such functionless and random arms.

We needed, and still need, what I once identified as the counterculture -an open-ended quest for all the brilliant ways humans can be. But somewhere in 1960's a dominant narrative in the counterculture undid the quest for extending higher living standards to the non-WASP's in the world, including blacks in the USA. Instead, the New Left and Postmodernists praised anything that undid Modernity, the undoing of anything Athena Techne. It became fashionable to encourage blacks, or any other marginalized non-white group, to stay ever more identified with their race and their original neighborhood, and their separate culture was superior and more beautiful than WASP America. The New Left and Postmoderns sought to divest blacks and other marginalized people of bourgeois aspirations. The Postmodern New Religious White

Right has only been too happy to oblige by working in other corridors of power to see those aspirations cut off by deregulation, wealth-by-pure-symbolic-manipulation, outsourcing and stagnating wages.

A better life is a human endeavor. Human endeavor is "Techne". The more we, of any race, continue down a road with Athena Techne in the rear-view mirror, the more dead ends we meet. Human agency is a root of manufactured risks, but risks are not undone by a baby playing with a match, risks are mitigated by Athena Techne. The baby with the match will just kill the whole family in the process of burning down civilization, and Lyotard should have known that, and we should know he is just Ares gathering up the forces of evil, to fight Athena Techne. In Greek mythology the poorest humans on Earth usually got it the worst when the Gods had their fights. Look out in the neighborhoods of the marginalized in America, and you will see those who suffered the reign of Ares in academia.

Chapter 4
Plebeian Tech Goddess Jolts Ivory Tower

Art intervenes when a boundary or limitation is recognized, and it creates a path that both transgresses and redefines that boundary. Fate and necessity may set temporary limits for invention, but their boundaries are perpetually redrawn by techne.

-Rhetoric reclaimed: Aristotle and the liberal arts tradition (Janet Atwill 1998)

At the age of nineteen I did field work in the Atchafalaya Basin as an engineer for a small telephone company. My job was to map and document every house within an "exchange". In the field of telecommunications, a telephone exchange or telephone switch is a system of electronic components that connects telephone calls. A central office is the physical building used to house equipment, especially telephone switches. These switches, automated and most of the time without humans on site, perform the same function telephone operators once did by connecting calls with a switchboard. We used the term "exchange" to refer to a geographical area served by a particular automated switching station.

We worked as a two-person team, driving down every road, including the most remote in an especially rural part of the state. The Atchafalaya Basin is the largest swampland in the United States, and also the heart of Cajun culture. In doing our job, we were also getting a thorough tour of backwoods Cajun life. Popular photos of the basin swampland are no exaggeration, it truly is a world of small parcels of land and lots of shallow water, and the further south you go the more water dominates, till your road is often the only consistent parcel of land in a sea of shallow marsh.

While doing our fieldwork for this area we stayed at the Sportsmen's Motel in Simmesport Louisiana. This was on the top edge of the triangle shaped Atchafalaya Basin. The Atchafalaya River begins at Simmesport, and from there going south starts to spread the environmental phenomenon called marsh, which in turn supports the Old French cultural phenomenon called Cajun.

The Mississippi River is close by Simmesport, the main tributary for the Atchafalaya. This may be radical news for some readers, but the Atchafalaya should actually be the new Mississippi River. The Atchafalaya would be, if humans had not built an elaborate system to keep the old Mississippi River where it is. This is because the big river switches to different routes about every thousand years. All of Southern Louisiana is only inches or feet above sea level, and small changes in land contour due to silt build up or erosion makes for a very dynamic river routing system. Some time after World War II the torrent of water coming off the Mississippi into the Atchafalaya should have become more than the water continuing on down to New Orleans. Morgan City should have become New Orleans 2.0, and original New Orleans could have become New Unemploymentland, a mix of alligators and abandoned buildings.

Nature's automation was to switch the incoming call of water from the northern Mississippi River, and route it through the center of Louisiana, but humans intervened, in order to save their previous investment of time and money. Along with time and money, lives: a local folk tale claims thousands of Irish immigrants died building the levees along the Mississippi around New Orleans.

The precarious situation for New Orleans, and the industrial development along the Mississippi from Simmesport to the Gulf, is a good example case for the Don't-Meddle-With-Nature narrative. But for the people living in southern Louisiana, building on and relying on the big river for economic opportunity is an imperative outsiders may not understand. Industrializing the river is how they pay for houses, cars, and hospitals. Hunting and fishing in the swamps provides protein for the dinner table, but people want something more than subsistence, and thus the control of the Mississippi becomes their burden in order to have a higher civilization.

Not all commitments to higher civilization are this precarious. The Earth is an uneven place, where in one place achieving or maintaining civilization is a great struggle and in another not so much. Keep in mind the lack of choice, and the precariousness, of subsistence cultures. Theirs is a flat Earth of less choice, of perennial determinism. Civilization is the aggregate effect of techne. Contrasted to subsistence cultures, techne is the crafting of choice.

If you, or your society, are at a dead end, you weren't doing your techne right.

That last statement is true, but overly simplistic for how civilization often plays out. Others can prevent you, or your society, from having the tools you need to craft a better situation. (Such as a prohibition on teaching a certain class how to read, or voting, or traveling.) But maybe this is the reason for Athena Techne carrying a spear, shield, thunderbolt and various symbols that imply wisdom. Fighting those who would block access to techne is a part of the game called civilization. It is the less civilized part, and in my opinion, is to be expected but not accepted.

Athena Techne provides the symbols and archetype to fight ones' way out of inequality. Besides the many tools she carries about in her life, her birth is also a lesson for those seeking emancipation. Metis was pregnant with Zeus' child. Zeus, being a typical paranoid and cruel King, knew his child could one day challenge him for his throne, just as he did his father Kronus, and set about to prevent such an end to his reign. He tricked Metis into making herself the size of a fly, he then swallowed her. Everything was fine for a while; till Zeus got an amazing headache, and had Hephaestus use his blacksmith tools to crack Zeus' head open. Athena burst forth from his forehead fully armed with weapons given by her mother.

So let's add to "If you, or your society, are at a dead end, you weren't doing your techne right" an extension: "If you are trapped by a cruel King, split their head open and come out fully matured and armed with every tool possible". Interestingly, this is not just crazy talk, it's a viable plan.

It was Plato's opinion that a philosopher-king would be the best kind of ruler. Zeus was the archetype of a self-protecting and violent despot. Combining these two rhetorical specimens into "philosopher-king as self-protecting and cruel despot" is an ideal jumping off point to the more general "rulership of an orthodoxy over the population". The orthodoxy can be one or all of a range of categories including religion, scientific theory, economic theory and practice, business models, military science or methodology, or even accepted styles of parenting. I'm generalizing with paradigm and encourage readers to think of a more practical and particular category in their lives.

Let's not be simple anti-authoritarians here. We should want society with structure, rituals, norms, leaders, and kudos to those who know more and get things done better, because without these things a society is formless and dissipates its gains. "Rulership of an orthodoxy over the population" isn't inherently wrong. Rather, what is wrong is when an old paradigm will not allow innovations to be heard or implemented. And even this is not wrong because of some sense of unfairness -all ideas should not get their day in the sun. We should not enable innovation and adaptability because we are nice, we should enable it because we want to survive.

There are intellectual terms for all this, from "epistemological rupture" to "paradigm shift". Such terms usually have a precise meaning and theatre of operation, but for us on the pop culture end of the spectrum the terms simply suggest a sweeping away of old ideas and replaced with new ones. I like this simple grasp, but do offer a cautionary tale of being too unguarded. Fascism has a kindred word: fashion, and that's what the fascist regimes of Germany and Italy were: the new fashion. We want to fashion something new, but introducing dark old ideas of one's race being the master race as part of a "new" fashion isn't really making anything new, innovative or good for civilization.

We have rhetorical snippets that can be mashed up to yield a framework for being true innovators, and being true liberators in the political sense. Postmodern thinker Jean-Francois Lyotard gave us the story of two people striking a match, one is an adult who strikes it for a purpose and with some boundaries for safety, and the second person is a toddler who strikes the match for no purpose, and the toddler's action is seen as an act of revolution against "the Establishment".

The toddler striking the match is not what we want, because we don't want civilization burned down, rather, we want ossified, corrupt, inefficient, needlessly unequal, and needless misery causing parts of "the Establishment" to be removed or rerouted around. We want to keep the house, with all its bourgeois aspirations, while removing the bad within it.

Within a specific scope of activity, if you have detailed knowledge, and are capable of skillful execution, you are a skilled public worker, what the Greeks called the *demiourgos*, literally "public worker", and which was originally a common noun meaning "craftsman" or "artisan". Later it was Latinized as 'demiurge', and took on more religious meaning related to forming and reshaping our world.

As shown earlier, we have some description of what the demiurge do in the following quotes:

> "*Every cause for a thing passing from not being to being is poiesis, so that manufacturing activities in all branches of industry are forms of poiesis and all artisans and craftsmen are poietai (poets).*" -The

Republic

> Techne is "*a capacity to do or make something with a correct understanding of the principle involved.*"
>
> -Aristotle

Rational has a root word: ratio. We all know what ratios are in math: 1/4 this element, 2/4 this other element, and 1/4 a final element. Why not rationalize (combine in a hybrid mix) Jean-Francois Lyotard's fire starting revolutionary toddler with the conservative sounding Aristotle's *capacity to do or make something with a correct understanding*. The new mix of the Lyotard radicalism and Aristotle's conservatism can be expressed as *Do or make something with skill, just not the way an authority figure, the inventor, or any predecessor would imagine or would condone*.

This hybrid is in a story we've all heard: The usurping of a technological power designed for one purpose, militancy and population control, and repurposed as the most powerful tool to undo militancy and control. It's the story of computers and the internet. You've read this celebratory narrative in lots of places before, and I can't emphasize enough how true and valuable it is. It's old (good) news, so I'll move on to a more tentative, darker tangent. It is a new problem for civilization, which arose because of the internet and computers.

The internetworking of financial trading, along with financial instruments that are circular, are new phenomena layered into civilization. It is causing wild oscillations in markets, with of course a result of misery on the ground for millions. Keep in mind this is not creative destruction -when an innovation emerges and all those too slow to switch to the new thing are losers. There is little being created when the fluctuations happen -so it is destruction without the word "creative" in front. A bizarre aspect in all this is money is made when the system fails (fails by the standards of pundits and laypeople), whether the numbers go up or down, there are some who profit whichever way a value moves. Volatility itself is putting money in their pocket. Once again: destruction without the word "creative" in front.

This is Jean-Francois Lyotard's fire starting toddler, from the most privileged and aristocratic family, burning down civilization and doing something Lyotard didn't imagine: getting more toys for it. Lyotard never imagined "the Establishment" striking the match. In the Bertrand Russell's Theory of Logical Types one can break the semantics of something by reusing it on itself. The aristocratic toddler world-burner seems like a complex example.

There is something you can do. And it is not filed under Communist or Revolutionary Anarchist. It is filed under *private property.* "Property" does not equate to "private property". "Private", if you look into the Latin roots, modifies to mean the intimate and personal. Ownership of something never intended for personal use or enjoyment is not private property. You have a private world, a world where you know intimate details about the behavior of the objects around you -their quirks, the way they operate best, and the way to maintain them.

Ares, the archetype of needless destruction, was famously stupid, a God who lost battles to smart and wily humans. I say the aristocratic toddler who is burning down civilization is an offshoot of Ares. He lacks knowledge of details, and (according to Lyotard, and worthy of praise from Lyotard) lacks skill and purpose. Sounds like an appropriate foe for Athena Techne, and her army of demiurge.

Water has something like a will, always falling from the sky or running downhill due to gravity. The Mississippi River has this in the form of a massive volition. Yet something that would not occur in nature, a dam, stops the big river from choosing its newer course down the Atchafalaya Basin. A human invention controls the Mississippi. Likewise inventions can control the demiurge, suppressing their crafting of choice. This is tantamount to ending innovation at the populist, distributed level. In such cases civilization becomes the lesser.

The people, the demiurge, have one thing in common with the Mississippi River -volition. The people also have something the river lacks - invention. It is by the powerful combined force of volition and invention that a civilization doesn't end due to one invention creating a wall that caged in and suppressed future lateral adaptations.

History is littered with societies that did not break out of the walls they created, and the civilization crumbled. Today the opportunity for failure is as present as ever. But civilization is forward morphic -it is something different today than it was in the past. The demiurge of today can route information to one another via the internet, and route physical gear to one another with next day shipping.

Individuals have ideas and gear -this is their private property. The ideas can be shared (copied) across the internet with other demiurge. The excess output from gear can be sold to other demiurge, and the gear itself can be resold on online marketplaces. A populist economy, or marketplace, emerges. But that is not the explosive news. The thing to be excited about is the absolutely new and utterly unpredictable things that will come into existence via recombination of what was once individual private property. Note this is not Soviet style sharing in which the society gives all output to the macro State, and the State distributes fairly, yielding a predictable, static and flat innovation spectrum. Rather, this is a strange social-ism that yields innovation through peer-to-peer trading of private property or sharing of ideas.

Today Athena Techne finds expression in the form of a tech savvy young woman who bought a solar power generation station for her home, has set up automated selling of excess electricity to the local microgrid, refurbished an almost free computer that uses entirely free software, her partner operates a metal fabrication shop in the garage, and they grow a stretch of tomatoes and corn on an abandoned lot across the street. She writes online blogs that share what works and what fails -from computer programs to a recipe for grilled tomatoes. Everything she uses she considers her private property, and ignores and undermines legal language that grants rights to her property to business entities far away. She has assigned herself primary law enforcement officer for the protection of herself and her property. She doesn't ask to be free or own what she owns. She considers herself a hacker, an entrepreneur, a fighter, and all these identities she thinks of as default roles of a homemaker.

A civilization made of such Athena's, aggressively owning and sharing, recombining their ideas and inventions, is a civilization capable of resilience.

I hope such Athena's are here, gestating in mighty Zeus' head, and ready to spring forth fully armed when the dam is burst.

Chapter 5
Towards Another Kind of Civilization

Throughout my youth and early adult life I was out of sync with the world around me. I didn't know how to align with other's values, methodologies or dialogue. I didn't know how to normalize.

I wasn't homeless, but at least could be called a vagabond. As an example, for a few years my Renault LeCar hauled me and all my stuff between fifteen-dollar-a-night Hotel La Acadian in Houma Louisiana to heliports from which I'd fly to oil rigs to wash dishes.

From 1982 to 2003 I didn't have a telephone.

Through my early adult life I worked hard, studied, and was a lot of other things that would have made an ideal citizen -but the good traits seemed to combine into something not very effective. It may have been because I worked hard on, or studied, or worried about things no one cared about. The ideas and projects in my head were hard work, but silly and useless on the open market. By accident, I chose one useless subject to read up on (useless in that time, and especially where I lived and worked) that panned out later: computers.

I took a few computer courses before 1995, mostly DOS courses. In 1995 something changed. My life, and I will argue, the course of civilization, dramatically changed. Everything changed when the hypertext protocol internet (http) became mainstream and ubiquitous. With email, making my own webpages, and seeking out the vast internet knowledgebase; I started becoming less of an utterly subjective and lone human, and more intertwined and enriched by the society and economy around me.

I went from ineffective drifter to a person with empowered mobility. In 1995 I was in Antarctica, and used the web to find a place that answered to every criteria I could imagine. The web answered back with "Seattle", and I'm now settled there and started a family. Throughout my life friends and family recommended places I might like to live, or recommended I stay in my hometown. The places were never a good match. With access to the internet, I put my criteria into a computer, and got back an answer that matched my head and my heart. Maybe the reason computers gave me more personable help can be found in Confucius' famous line "man is not a machine", also translated as "man is not a utensil". My friends and family are not my utensil, they embed themselves into any dialogue, including answers to questions about what I should do with my life. A computer can be a utensil, void of injecting its preferences into a reply. Or maybe the computer *did* embed its preferences: it recommended I move to Seattle, a place computers like to live and work.

I arrived in Seattle on the Empire Builder passenger train on November 1, 1996. I checked into a room at the YMCA, and started a walk around the city to get oriented. I walked straight through Belltown, up Queen Anne hill, back down to South Lake Union, Capitol Hill, and then took Roosevelt Avenue over to the University District. On my first day I had walked most of the inner city, and knew it well enough to shop for an apartment.

While in Antarctica I had discovered Seattle's Speakeasy Cafe and Network. As of 2010 it's a rather progressive internet service provider, but in 1996 it was so much more -they had a large cafe with Unix machines, art gallery, music performance space, coffee and beer. One website titled "Caustic Compendium", created by a Speakeasy user, and hosted on speakeasy.org, was an indispensable introduction to Seattle's secretive hip culture. This website gave me insights that would've never been manifest by walking down the streets of Seattle.

On my second day ever in Seattle, I walked into the Speakeasy Cafe at 2304 2nd Ave in Belltown (downtown Seattle) and signed up for a Unix shell account. This came with 10MB of user disk space, email account accessed using PINE (Program for Internet News & Email, developed locally at UW), and free use of text-only VT100 style terminals and access at all RAIN sites (Remote Access Internet Nodes). The RAIN sites were all over the city, at independent espresso cafes, such as Cafe Allegro in the U District.

There were twelve VT100 terminals at the Speakeasy Cafe, and two at Cafe Allegro. I loved those terminals. The pleasure was in the combination ambient of two spaces I was operating in at the same time: 1) the sights. sounds and culturally overloaded/overclocked meaning of the cafes; 2) the black background and green letters and numbers of the text-only Unix command line with no graphics other than text and a blinking green square that marks the current input.

But the world moves on, and when in it does, something is deleted. The Speakeasy Cafe burned down the night of May 18, 2001 at 10:10

PM. I wasn't there, but tales of the fire are ironic and scary. The theme of the evening's music and poetry readings was "fire and brimstone", in remembrance of the May 18 eruption of Mount St. Helens in 1980. The cafe had about fifty people inside, including a few toddlers. The fire alarm was disconnected because of construction on the second floor. A few patrons had just happened to be outside and saw smoke, and alerted those insides. They all quickly exited, but were thinking it was a small fire easily put out and they'd go back inside. Within a couple of minutes cars parked along the street were having their paint cooked off, and the building was in a total dramatic blaze. The cafe never reopened.

I had moved on before the demise of the Speakeasy Cafe. In the summer of 2000 I spent a month living at Seattle's Fishermen's Terminal aboard the P/B Neptune, a fish processing barge, preparing my laboratory for testing the quality of ikura (salmon eggs). I had my Linux computer on board the boat, and had wireless internet access through a Ricochet modem. I would still telnet into a Speakeasy Unix shell account while a "live aboard". The boat had a crazy crew, full of characters like "Felony Mike", "Big Daddy", and the best leader I've ever worked for: Brett Van Zandt (twin brother of the aforementioned "Big Daddy"). Half Norwegian and Native American, these twins were also the loudest, roughest voiced, and most cuss word using humans I've ever encountered.

In June we took the barge to Alaska, and I spent two months as head of quality control on the boat. I came back with a cool ten thousand dollars, and moved on campus at The Evergreen State College, a little college of four thousand students nestled in an old growth forest on the outskirts of Olympia Washington.

At Evergreen I completed my Bachelor of Science in 2003. Along the way I did projects in Lisp, Perl, PHP and Java programming languages. I went on to be a white-collar engineer type, writing programs or testing computer performance. The internet was no longer just a play space for personal indulgence; it was now a place for me to work for a paycheck. The internet became less like educational television and more like the gritty, mean, and real streets we use to get to work, go to a friend's house, gather for a political rally, or go shopping. The same thoroughfare used by crooks going to a home invasion, abduction, or bank robbery.

...or space in which to conduct a war.

While at Evergreen I got to thinking of myself as a radical. My first foray into this was as a volunteer for *indymedia.org*, an early giant in alternative media that sprang into existence to report on the anti W.T.O. protests in Seattle 1999. Volunteering in of itself was not so provocative. Going to indymedia.org's Seattle office for orientation while an FBI van with audio surveillance was sitting in the alley eavesdropping; that was at least *intended* to be provocative.

Months later I finally angered someone in authority, one who had very high-level access to government databases on civilians. I posted on *seattle.indymedia.org* what I thought was an amateurish idea for getting text communication past government surveillance, by placing the text in a GIF or JPG, then emailing the file as an attachment. I woke up the next morning, and someone had posted a reply with most of my family's names and cities they lived in, some exact street addresses. They also said I should abandon promoting the text communication idea.

In January 2004 I received an email from the Director of Communications for the Communist Party of the USA (CPUSA). He had been reading my online political essays, liked my ideas, and offered to pay for a trip to the CPUSA headquarters in New York City. Specifically, he wanted my participation in a conference focused on defeating George Bush in the next Presidential election. I went there, had an intellectually invigorating experience, and also a very intimate stay in Manhattan and Brooklyn including gazing out the CPUSA Headquarters window at the beautiful and spooky Chelsea Hotel just across the street.

But the CPUSA was not my most radical extreme. Months after the trip to CPUSA headquarters, I picked up *The Culture of Make Believe* by Derrick Jensen. I got so infatuated with Jensen's ideas I joined an email list, sort of an inner circle of believers in his agenda. I even had a brief correspondence with Jensen, to help him fix his computer. I eventually discovered he, and his followers, don't just see civilization collapsing and humans reverting to a much simpler lifestyle -Jensen has written other books recommending the violent destruction of civilization via such things as blowing up river dams. Today I see Jensen, his values, thesis and agenda as void of anything valid.

What ties this odd list of life experiences together was the internet as the point of contact. The less obvious common feature was immobility and relative poverty. In those years I was a poor college student stuck in Olympia. It's as if restless energy, not having an outlet in travel and adventure, found an outlet through politicized internet activity.

"Politicized internet activity" is so cheap, the materials needed are already lying around (a computer or text messaging cellphone), and a little practice is all that is needed to make an Improvised Rhetorical Device. This morning, for example, while waiting for caffeine to kick in I created a graphic to promote a certain provocative free speech event coming up in May (I'm omitting specifics here for self-protection, and anonymity is part of the power of this particular action anyway) , uploaded the graphic to a free web server, and posted a link to the image on an internationally famous website forum. There is a slight possibility this IRD may blow up (offend) enough people it makes the evening news within the target cultural group by the following evening.

Improvised Rhetorical Devices and Improvised Explosive Devices have defined the early 21st century. Foreign and domestic government policies, even corporate policies, are shaped by the threat of these devices. The goal of those who create these devices is system disruption. System disruption is understood by those furthest from ivory towers of political/military theory, by those at the base of the political pyramid. It's most simple instance could be called sabotage, but the same action, if done at the right point in a system, at a crossroads of several system layers, can become the much more advanced instance: a hit on a systempunkt.

The term systempunkt was coined and published by fourth generation war theorist John Robb in December 2004.

- Systempunkts are identified by distributed, autonomous groups comprised of commoners rather than a central command comprised of elites.
- A Systempunkt is a point at the crossroads of several system layers.
- A Systempunkt is a point within a infrastructure or market system.
- The goal of an attack is to cause a cascade of collapse in the targeted system.
- Target system: Infrastructure: successful attack disrupts flows that result in immediate financial loss or ongoing supply shortages.
- Target system: Market: successful attack destabilizes the psychology of the market and induces severe inefficiencies and uncertainties.

It may be good to double back and reassert something: the book you are holding is about Athena Techne, Goddess of Civilization, Technology, and Wisdom. This book desires the thriving of civilization, technology and wisdom. This book is a systempunkt designed to fight other systempunkts; to fight those who want less civilization, technology and wisdom. It is a device of advanced warfare, aimed at enemy instances of advanced warfare.

Athena had a few weapons associated with her personage -a spear, a shield with the head of Medusa attached, and lightning bolts. Civilization, a protectorate of Athena, has another weapon: **collapse**.

Yes, collapse. The very thing haters of civilization and technology seek after is the very thing that could undermine their efforts and agenda. The Zombies of Ares - whether they are nature nihilists such as Derrick Jensen and the Earth Liberation Front, Islamic extremists, or racial-solidarity gangs - these actors (and their supporters) often consider their activities as chipping away at the bedrock of a system they hold in contempt. Here is how that system - whether you call it civilization, the bourgeoisie, or industrialized culture- could turn terrorist's and criminal's activity into a strengthening mechanism, and consume them and or their resources.

Incorporation of disturbance (Ahl & Allen 1996) is how collapse can empower, if it is done just so.

1. Disturbance is a force that comes from outside the target system.

2. After a disturbance the target system is modified. Its internal processes register some change in reaction to the disturbance.

3. Modification will fit in one of these categories:

   A. Greatly change=>Negative=>Dead.
   B. Slightly changed=>
   Indecisive=>Recurrence of similar disturbance may send to negative or positive result.
   C. Greatly changed=>Positive=>Resilient, hardy, capable of surviving similar disturbances indefinitely. Often due to new internal processes that depend upon and/or consume resources provided by the recurring disturbance. (e.g. Forest and tree types that use fire disturbance as positive effect on regeneration and hygiene.)

4. Iteration of the above.
   Disturbance =>A. or B. or C. =>Disturbance..

This is *incorporation of disturbance,* not as popular as *competition* when discussing evolution, which is unfortunate, since competition is overrated as a stimulant for change. Competition has a conservative effect on change, it is even resistant to change due its removal of aberrant individuals. Disturbance, in contrast, always produces change (Ahl & Allen 1996).

Systempunkts rely on our modern, centralized-production form of civilization for a target. The people behind the systempunkts are decentralized, scattered from the remote regions of Waziristan to the sprawl of American suburbs. If the terrorists' target is centralized industrial civilization, remove the target, then even the greatest aim will not hit it.

Those who hate enough to attempt destroying civilization almost always see a bygone era as better. I've known hundreds who believe mankind around ten thousand years ago was the best, and they hope to spray graffiti, vandalize restaurant bathrooms, or burn down new housing projects till we are back in the Stone Age (I have dozens if not hundreds of personal experiences hearing advocacy of this since being in the Northwest US). Conservative and extreme Islamists want what they once had in the Middle Ages -a Caliph unchallenged by European and Chinese political leverage, and also expansion of Islamic hegemony into southern Europe and China's western edge.

Five hundred years from now, progressive civilization is likely to still have these same threats emerging every other generation.

To love or defend civilization, technology and progress is to never love or defend a bygone era. We must be in love with, and fend for, the capacity for change. I am not claiming we should change for the sake of change itself. The rate of change doesn't mark a better culture, it is the capacity for iterative improvement that marks a greater advantage.

Japan in the 19th century is an excellent example. They were excellent metalworkers -even had the first ironclad navy during their warring states period- but their metalwork largely focused on sword making. They were not an industrialized economy. Yet when globalization (rudely) met their shores, they quickly mastered industrialization, converting their material culture to amongst the most modern on the planet. The Japanese, at that moment before they industrialized, are a great example of latent capacity for change.

In this year that I write this book we are standing on the antecedent edge of potential much like the agrarian Japanese just before they leapt to modernization. This potential new era has been summed up by writer John Robb with the phrase "***Localize production, virtualize everything else***".

Before we leap forward, I'd like to look back to relate weak points in the past. I recall television advertisements in the early 1970's that accidently capture a weakness in 20th century America. These ads would say something like "If they can put a man on the moon, you'd think they could make instant coffee that tastes good". This was a folksy way of referring to the vast cadre of research facilities run by corporations and the federal government, for instance I.B.M., Bell Labs, and NASA. People (non-engineer common folks) expected these research giants to churn out solutions and improvements to our daily lives, such as better coffee or flying cars with video telephones. We, the common folks, were not supposed to know how the stuff worked, we just made sure we had a good job, saved our money up then bought the "product".

The weakness in this great but aging culture of the 20th century was the distance between the common folk and the engineers who worked at the research facilities. The common folk rarely learned or mastered the details. And remember, a lack of propensity for details is a tendency of Zombies who work for Ares (see Chapter 2). I am not saying common non-engineering folk are something as extreme as evil, rather, I am saying if a population doesn't know how their stuff works -the very stuff they rely on- then a lack of control and agency becomes the norm. Lack of control and agency is the very seed of human misery.

Today we have lack of control and agency over what matters: the complex objects in our material culture. Common folk are sold the idea their vote in democratic elections are the ultimate control of destiny, and often vote with a focus on meta criteria such as how liberal or conservative the politician is. All the while things in the person's life -such as internet connection speed, or reliability and fuel economy of the cars they have to choose from; these products may play a greater role in their economic viability than having as their political representative an actor who pretends to be a like-minded person. This is the "democracy" Americans practiced during the 20th century -an era rife with Zombies on TV, serving their murderous god Ares.

Democracy has not always been on TV. In its earliest days, originating in the same city that claimed Athena as its guide and protector, democracy was more direct. The term "direct" is the very opposite of "mediate", and "mediate" relies on "media", one of which is television. Every television that is on is one less instance of direct, Athenian, democracy.

I don't want to commit the same error as those who believe in a *Golden Age*. There is a tendency of the mind to assume some bygone era was perfect, or close to perfect, and as time goes on the perfection is slowly decomposing and distorting into imperfection -the Genesis story of perfection in the Garden, the Chinese perfect dynasty as the origin of their Empire, anarcho-primitivist's belief that humans had a higher living standard before settling into agrarian villages and cities- the spell of Golden Age-ism can cloud the historical views of religious and secular alike. So it is with the origins of democracy.

Athens certainly had direct democracy, but there was a catch. We all know in the late 20th century society had access to roads, but the only ones who could use them were those with a driver's license and a legally operating vehicle - likewise with the voting scene in Athens. Some estimates claim the city had 250,000 inhabitants, and around 30,000 had voting rights, and then of those only 5,000 had the time or ability to attend assemblies regularly.

I've had personal experience with this is sort "open to the public" that is not really timed to be open to the public. I especially remember a Seattle city design conference in which the organizers were plastering their promotional material with gleeful claims of being a public forum, a chance for the community to influence the creation of their environment. The devil was in the details: it was scheduled for two weekdays during business hours. This meant those in city bureaucratic positions specific to urban design, urban design students, and professionals from the major land developers of urban Seattle, such as Vulcan Inc. could easily attend. I couldn't.

Only 5,000 Athenians consistently pulling the levers of governance, and my experience with my city's urban design blocked by the soft barrier of inconvenience. These examples could lead one to the conclusion: ***elite oligarchy is an unbendable law of human nature.***

Human nature, allow me to introduce to you technology. Technology may be just the companion to bend a previously unbendable law. Human nature is just a specific subset of a wider phenomenon called biological life. Humans developed technology in the pursuit of survival, and late 20th and early 21st century technology is starting to have things in common with biological life. *Information: A Very Short Introduction* by Luciano Floridi (Oxford University Press, 2010) offers a definition of biological life as any *entity that works against entropy by embodying information-processing operations in service to their own survival or reproduction*.

Humans now have technologies that embody information-processing operations. These objects are everywhere on Earth humans are - cellphones are so common in shanty-towns of the third world their prepaid calling cards function as currency. Computers, cellphones and robots don't fend for their own survival or reproduce, but they certainly do extract and react to information from their environment. Here is where it gets good for humans: the anti-entropy of a technological object isn't by default focused on itself, but rather provides its behaviors in service to its human companions and operators.

To give a plain, simple, and full example: a global positioning capable cellphone can extract and react to its environment to provide its user, a lost hiker, directions back to safety. The cellphone does not decide to leave the user behind in the woods, and march out to save itself - which is what it could do if it was a true form of biological life.

Technology that embodies information-processing operations, in the form of handheld and tabletop sized devices -are everywhere, in everyone's hands. Extremely powerful and multiplicative forms of anti-entropy, a.k.a. survival options, are available to everyone. This is a new stage in human history.

In the pursuit of a new kind of civilization, a root cause of that civilization will be access to a larger variety of anti-entropic behaviors than citizens of 20th century America, or ancient Athens, had. "***Localize production, virtualize everything else***" is a modality that circumvents the entropic snares laid by the parasite team of human nature: elite oligarchs and their companions: apathetic unimaginative folk.

Earlier I mentioned collapse as a weapon to use against those who want to end civilization. These terrorists and nihilists target the elite oligarchs, the apathetic common folk, and the proactive common folk as one. Civilization could collapse up to a more complex and resilient form of itself if the proactive common folk stepped out of the target. States and centralized industry (owned by elite oligarchs) would then receive the systempunkts. The proactive folk would already be stepping over into the new "***Localize production, virtualize everything else***" civilization, which by definition would be providing the things state services and centralized industry once did, and also benefiting from weakened or less relevant elite oligarchs, and finally in a cultural modality with no niche for elite oligarchs.

What does this look like? In the closing of Chapter 4 we saw someone doing this new kind of civilization:

Today Athena Techne finds expression in the form of a tech savvy young woman who bought a solar power generation station for her home, has set up automated selling of excess electricity to the local microgrid, refurbished an almost free computer that uses entirely free software, her partner operates a metal fabrication shop in the garage, and they grow a stretch of tomatoes and corn on an abandoned lot across the street. She writes online blogs that share what works and what fails -from computer programs to a recipe for grilled tomatoes. Everything she uses she considers her private property, and ignores and undermines legal language that grants rights to her property to business entities far away. She has assigned herself primary law enforcement officer for the protection of herself and her property. She doesn't ask to be free or own what she owns. She considers herself a hacker, an entrepreneur, a fighter, and all these identities she thinks of as default roles of a homemaker.

A civilization made of such Athena's, aggressively owning and sharing, recombining their ideas and inventions, is a civilization capable of resilience. I hope such Athena's are here, gestating in mighty Zeus' head, and ready to spring forth fully armed when the dam is burst.

Chapter 6
At the 100th Meridian, Facing the High Plains, We Started Towards Outer Space

Once I was in a doctor's waiting room, and picked up a magazine with a very interesting article. The article offered that when Freudian and feminist views turn into an epistemology (explaining everything humans create or do), they become impervious to invalidation, because anyone not agreeing with the Freudian or feminist explanatory lens is obviously duped and corrupted by the very mentalities Freudian or feminists critique and see beyond. True believers. Atheists claim religious people have blinders on, and serve a limited explanatory view of the universe. Seems the potential of being duped by one's own symbolism is just as possible among secular professionals and religious laypeople alike. Maybe we think moving from a narrow, small town to the bigger smarter city, and settling there, is emancipation, when all the while we should be moving from the small town to bigger smarter cities, and then moving on if need be. True nomads.

I was in the waiting room scheduled to see a NASA psychologist. I had just made it through thirteen months in Antarctica, and NASA considered us "winter-overs" the closest in experience to long-term space travel. NASA wanted to discover what types of people survived the Antarctica winter with the least social and psychological problems, and hoped to use that data to help design a better astronaut. A NASA doctor had flown to McMurdo Station, Antarctica to see any of us who wanted to volunteer for an interview. It was a more honest test to interview us while still under the stress and in the context.

The interview was uneventful; the doctor said I seemed to have done well. I had, with one notable exception we didn't discuss. I had fallen for this girl who worked in my department, and also wintered over. She wasn't interested in me romantically. She offered her friendship, but that's it. I made it really rough on myself that winter, with all kinds of unrequited-love issues going through my head. We are still friends on an online social network. She's a good person, and I was the confused person back through that winter. Since then I discovered a pattern, and it has something to do with attractive girls, but more to do with a type of land and climate.

In each case I was in a markedly elevated state of happiness, levitated by land and climate that made my mind and body function better than wherever I had previously been in. In one case it was going from Arkansas to the high altitudes of northern Arizona, New Mexico, Utah, and Wyoming. In another it was going from the Amish farm country around Lancaster, Pennsylvania to Antarctica. In all cases I had moved from a land rich in water and able to grow food easily (Eden), and had entered a place that offered little or no potential for farming or living off the land (Not Eden). The Not Edens had won me over with their rugged and austere beauty, and less humid air. The Edens were miserable in the summer, and the land was rarely inspiring -it took interesting buildings and highways to make Edens invigorating and attractive.

What's odd is my associating the positive euphoria of the Not Edens with the nearest attractive female, confusing the woman and the environment, and falling in love with both as one package. I may never fully understand why such a convoluted mismanagement of my emotions occurred. Maybe it was the taboo territory I was venturing into. Society -through movies like Avatar, scriptural stories like Genesis, green political advocacy and plain old conversation- had represented rich garden-like lands as desirable, as the default aspiration. I was abandoning what these messages around me had ascribed as the properly desirable object: a place with Eden-like qualities. Maybe I was afraid of becoming an outsider, and alone, by having sentiments that did not agree with the dominant paradigm, and latched onto the nearest (attractive) accomplice in my quest out of Eden.

Whatever. I freaking hate hot, humid places cluttered with trees.

For the Genesis story to work, we are supposed to like the idea of living in the Garden. What about those who break that narrative's assumptions, as I do, by preferring lands without abundant food, water, and warmth? For us, hiking around the summit of Mount Olympus is heavenly, living forever in an oasis of the Fertile Crescent is hell. I didn't mention Fertile Crescent oasis on mere whim, this has everything to do with the Garden of Eden. The story of the Garden is remarkably similar to what an oasis in the deserts of the Middle East and Africa are like: plenty of fruit bearing plants, water, and the weather is right for no need of clothes. What is the most likely naturally occurring threat that could chase occupants out into the desert? A large serpent (which is a prominent character in the Garden of Eden story). But as I said, there are those of us who would leave the oasis without the prompting of a serpent or angry God.

The Garden was an ancient Middle Eastern storytelling invention, bearing some of the unique contours of land and climate of the Arabian Peninsula and Africa. Mankind certainly suffered a "Fall" –the fall was when this cancer of a story exported to Europe and also became the reward afterlife in Islam.

Pagan Greek origin stories point to a beginning composed of Chaos (formlessness), from which order, and a narrative emerge with the first deities, Gaia and Eros, then a lineage of gods and mortals giving a sense of progress and hierarchy. The stories are a little inconsistent due to many variations by oral storytellers, but these inconsistencies enrich with an organic irregularity. Eventually the pantheon introduces Athena. Unlike Eve, Athena doesn't enter the story nude, unaware of good and evil, and without technology. Rather, Athena springs forth fully grown, armed, clothed, and wise. Her equipment, including her mental equipment of cunning and calculation, implies the world she is inserted into is already warring and corrupt.

She doesn't oppose these vices by working to end civilization -to take it back to an idyllic primitive state or on to a heavenly conclusion- rather she works to preserve civilization through both mental and technological invention.

When discussing individuals, we say they can keep themselves fresh and invigorated by self-expansion, such as exploring new places, acquiring skills in a new hobby, job or language. This is what civilization itself needs to do, and does all the time. Self-expansion is what humans do better than animals -we invent such things as wheels, ship canals, and many genres of poetic verse to battle entropy and vice. Self-expansion is civilization. Civilization is self-expansion.

In the story of Adam and Eve, self-expansion was a sin, and among a many in green politics, civilization is a sin against "natural heritage". These political inhibitions and religious prohibitions erroneously masked as innocence and righteousness are a bane to empowerment, with the biggest losers being those trying to work their way out of immobility, poverty and ignorance.

It took self-expansion in the form of travel and desert camping, even a summer of home being a 1991 Ford Fiesta, to discover the difference between inhibited Eden and lands of paradise. In my youth, I hadn't traveled far enough, only seeing the world in an arc of Interstate highway connections between Houston Texas and Waterbury Connecticut, with most of my life spent in Little Rock. Then I drove through the 100th meridian, into the western half of North America.

The 100th meridian is a line going from the North Pole to the South Pole, and travels through the middle of North America. It is the line that divides the humid and well-watered eastern US from the dryer air and less water sources of the high altitude plains, deserts, and Rocky Mountains of the western US.

I first experienced the Great Plains on a solo road trip in 1992, on Interstate 40 from Little Rock, Arkansas to New Mexico. I felt a never-before sense of physical comfort at about Amarillo, where the elevation is 3600 feet. The beautiful table-top flat and treeless grasslands gave way to an even prettier desert rock and mountains of New Mexico. I phoned my parents from a roadside stop in a state of euphoria.

I pressed on to White Sands National Monument, and my first camping trip in desert sand dunes. From my campsite I could see the mountain ranges that run north-south on both sides of the basin. Less than 100 miles north of me in the same desert basin was the site of the first atomic bomb detonation.

My little tent home was paradise. I was a high plains nomad, worshipping the nighttime display of war objects of the sky (there are almost constant top-secret tests at the missile range, ironically a non-secret and viewable to the naked eye).

The Indo-European Kurgan tribes were nomadic pastoralists, and worshipped deities remote from Earth -Sky Gods. 6,000 years ago, the Sky God worshippers came out of the high plains of south-central Asia and overran the Earth Gods residing with or caring for plants, animals and rivers. The Sky God worshippers were more war-like (or at least war-capable by being horseback riders) than the worshippers of Earth Gods. Sky God worshippers overran Europe, and during the migrations out of Europe around 800 B.C., also overran Anatolia, Iran and India.

In late 20th century America there began to be an awareness of the Sky God versus Earth God distinction, usually with those aware of the distinction expressing preference for Earth God cultural traits. A criticism of Sky God cultures (e.g. Islam, Christianity) suggests the deities are removed from earthly concerns and feelings, this estrangement ultimately resulting in a contemptuous treatment of the living. Even though Earth God worshippers make me real tired, I think this Sky God criticism is largely valid.

Athena is a unique point on the Sky Gods versus Earth Gods map. As opposed to other

Earth God types, she is more tied to skills and activities of humans, rather than patron of animals, plants and earth. As opposed to Sky God types, she is a patron of things that go on in our world, not in heaven or Platonic Forms. Sky Gods for sure meddle in human affairs. There are examples of bringing down kingdoms, upbraiding a single person, and making food appear miraculously. But most of these heavenly interventions are some sort of special effect -the normal flow of events, or physics of the universe, are interrupted by divine will and something is saved or destroyed in odd fashion. Athena, on the other hand, works within the normal process of metalwork, military strategy, and legislative/jurisprudence process. She gave Athens olive oil for its utility in everyday needs, rather than waving a wand and making belly's full and lamps provide a fuel-less light.

You don't ask Athena to end a scourge of mice; you enlist her persona by inventing a better mousetrap.

We have Sky Gods versus Earth Gods. Amongst Earth God paganism and polytheism why not add the distinction of Biological Paganism versus Geological Paganism?

Most pagans I know in contemporary Seattle focus on the raw forces of Mother Nature as the divine. Not just raw forces like wind across the Dry Lakes of Antarctica, their focus is almost all biological, with the celestial and seasonal being an exception, though the celestial and seasonal is a punctuation focused on biological effects on crops or humans.

Geological Paganism would focus on minerals, not life. Not a worship of a sample of gypsum, but recognition of the awe and grandeur of objects such as buildings, automobiles, bridges, towers, ships, Rocky Mountains, sand covered deserts, and planets. All these things have in common a mineral composition and geological explanation, and they are not alive (living systems are any anti-entropic informational entity). By geological explanation I mean they are physical matter that have been moved and shaped into something we can name and classify, and they maintain that structure for a meaningful duration of time. For instance, a mountain, building, or metal fork stays structurally the same for some time meaningful for human purpose. Also, the objects of veneration in Geological Paganism can be mined, or are a product of mining.

According to a view amongst geologists, humans are amongst the greatest geological forces on the planet, extracting massive amounts of planetary materials and shipping them all over the globe, even into outer space in the form of satellites or space stations. Road construction (the extracting of stone, grinding it, and then relaying it as a road) alone has reshaped the planet. Fusion of manmade and natural geological specimens provides a functional language to express Geological Paganism.

Geological Paganism is an umbrella term for an aesthetic. There are many, like myself, who are stirred to the point of awe by the view of mountains, valleys shaped by glacier, ocean, skyscrapers, wide expanses of desert rock, the hum of semi rigs on an Interstate highway, and the blinking lights of communication towers at night. To divide this list into natural and manmade might serve an academic or political objective, but at the aesthetic level it would be a lie to say the natural is beautiful and the manmade is not. They are one experience, and one awe.

While writing this book, I've made frequent visits to the office spaces of City of Seattle government. The office space, court rooms, and conference space are a "campus" of three buildings with 5th Ave. and Cherry St. as their common intersection. It is impressive to see the effective spread of a mass psychosis throughout. Paintings, sculptures, government program posters, and other messages have a consistent explicit text or implicit subtext in which the manmade is ugly and natural heritage is revered.

For me, this is a sad and needless civil war amongst ourselves. It is especially disconcerting to see those who craft and implement city design to be serving such a psychotic denial of the grandeur and beauty that is Seattle -the whole Seattle captured on popular postcards with skyscrapers, Highway 99, the industrial cranes along the port, Elliot Bay and mountains in the background.

The threats of Zombies of Ares are perennial, and Athena Techne's mental and physical equipment has prepared her, and civilization, to prevail. Those who would subtract the manmade -first from their personal list of beautiful things, then from the environment around them- are reconfiguring their own selves in the process. They are un-equipping, and humans fundamentally rely on equipment to endure.

Geological Paganism taps into emotional attachments and aesthetics more likely west of the 100th meridian, and more likely after the proliferation of metal and concrete. The more sparse distribution of plants helps geology come to the fore, whereas in the more biologically dense eastern side of the meridian plant life hides or obscures geology. We can trace the presence of those with Geological Pagan aesthetics in the east by the history of removing plant life and erecting cities and highways, the Geological Pagans were reshaping a land dominated by biology into a land dominated by geology, to serve their perfectly legitimate aesthetics.

At an emblematic and iconic level the skyline of New York City serves as reference to Geological Paganism on the eastern side North America, and the Grand Canyon does the same for the western side. Techne in the east, and physis in the west. Of course we don't have to be so slavishly centralized -the eastern icon could be Boston, Toronto, the elevated subways of Chicago; and likewise in the west it could the Grand Tetons, Bryce Canyon, or Half-Dome.

One of the earliest pushes past the 100th meridian, involving exploration and a significant amount of migration and settlement, is the Mormon discovery of the Salt Lake Valley. This is not a story of the simple and foolhardy who endure a land lacking in water and plentiful in rattlesnakes. It is a story of methodical and scientific explorers -much like on Star Trek, in which Orson Pratt stars as Spock and Brigham Young stars as Captain James T. Kirk. These explorers -being of numerate, literate and scientific predisposition- kept meticulous logs of their travels.

The initial starship that blasted off from Winter Quarters heading through the 100th Meridian towards what is now called Utah was a multi-vessel configuration called *The Vanguard Company*.

Quantification follows.

Vanguard Company = {
143 men.
3 women.
2 children.
73 wagons.
1 cannon.
93 horses.
52 mules.
66 oxen.
19 cows.
17 dogs.
1 map based on John Fremont's western expedition.
Instruments for calculating: latitude,
elevation,
temperature,
barometric pressure.
… and some chickens. }

Blast off was April 5, 1847 at 2 p.m. A few weeks into the journey the company scribe, William Clayton -assigned with measuring speed and distance, by counting wagon wheel revolutions- began to tire of his job and wanted to design a mechanism to do the work for him. Clayton consulted with mathematician Orson Pratt, and subsequently designed the first odometer.

On July 21, 1847 scouts of the company entered the Salt Lake Valley. Two days later irrigation ditches began to be constructed, turnips and potatoes were planted, the next day after that saw the dedication for the site of a future temple to their God, and a city plan was put on paper.

Introduction of non-native plants, terraforming, an epistemology normalizing hub (religious temple), and intended urban replacement of wildlands -anathema to nature worshipping nihilists, but an exemplary instance of bootstrapping Athena Techne.

The Mormons had an evolutionary pressure on them before this exploration past the 100th meridian began -Missouri Governor Lilburn Boggs issued an extermination order against all Mormons living in the state. The Mormons were driven from Eden, into a no man's land without developed infrastructure nor the protection and encouragement of government.

…and they made a paradise.

This could be a template story for our exploration and settlement on other planets and moons of outer space. Those predisposed of numerate, literate and scientific methodologies may be chased out of their original homeland called Earth by the Zombies of Ares (typified in this story by Missouri Governor Lilburn Boggs), and thrust out to find a surprising paradise in cave shelters of the Moon or metal containers on Mars.

Geological Pagans have an advantage -they like rock, they like metal. A trade-off, leaving behind culinary arts, taxes, and death on Earth, replaced by rock and ice strewn worlds, fabricated food, and metal bedrooms, is likely an appealing offer to Geological Pagans, while a horrific consideration for Biological Pagans and tradition bound Sky God worshippers.

In chapter five I wrote on collapse as an evolutionary leap for civilization. Collapse being ***"Localize production, virtualize everything else"*** -a decline of centralized authority and industrialization, replaced by localized authority and industrialization. Popular assumptions may consider space exploration one of the activities only big governments can do, and if we collapse to an end of centralized power such as big governments and mega-corporations, then quests into outer space will be over.

Freeman Dyson disagrees with this popular assumption. Dyson is a British-American theoretical physicist and mathematician, famous for his work in quantum field theory, solid-state physics, and nuclear engineering. From 1957 to 1961 he worked on the Orion Project, which proposed the possibility of space-flight using nuclear pulse propulsion. A prototype was demonstrated using conventional explosives, but a treaty which he was involved in and supported, banned the testing of nuclear weapons other than underground, and this caused the project to be abandoned.

Freeman Dyson references the Mormon migration to Utah while discussing space exploration or settlement:

> *"I've done some historical research on the costs of the Mayflower's voyage, and on the Mormons' emigration to Utah, and I think it's possible to go into space on a much smaller scale. A cost on the order of $40,000 per person [1978 dollars] would be the target to shoot for; in terms of real wages, that would make it comparable to the colonization of America.*

> *Unless it's brought down to that level it's not really interesting to me, because otherwise it would be a luxury that only governments could afford."*

Regarding the slow pace of space exploration by United States government programs, Dyson remarks:

> *"The problem is, of course, that they can't afford to fail. The rules of the game are that you don't take a chance, because if you fail, then probably your whole program gets wiped out".*

Contrast is pronounced when Dyson speaks of his faith in small groups separately working on a similar problem:

> *"...the amusing thing is that it really doesn't matter whether we succeed or not, because there are hundreds of other little groups like us around the world. One or another is going to come up with the right idea, and it's no tragedy if ours fails."*

To sum up the lack of impediments humanity has for going into outer space, Dyson offered these encouraging words:

> *"No law of physics or biology forbids cheap travel and settlement all over the solar system and beyond. But it is impossible to predict how long this will take. Predictions of the dates of future achievements are notoriously fallible. My guess is that the era of cheap unmanned missions will be the next fifty years, and the era of cheap manned missions will start sometime late in the twenty-first century".*

(A quote used previously on page 50, Ch. 4:) *Art intervenes when a boundary or limitation is recognized, and it creates a path that both transgresses and redefines that boundary. Fate and necessity may set temporary limits for invention, but their boundaries are perpetually redrawn by techne (Atwill 1998).* Athena Techne, working within human endeavor, has brought civilization to this point, breaking barriers of entropy all along the way. The pattern is established, and we should have faith it will repeat again. It will, as long as our faith accompanies desire and action, rather than contentment and passivity.

Chapter 7
It is the business of the future to be dangerous

In April 2000 I was sitting at my Linux computer in a tiny basement apartment on 52nd Street in Seattle [the closet sized apartment on the northeast corner of the house at 1310 NE 52nd St, Seattle, WA 98105, USA, the other basement apartment was occupied by Crunchbird guitarist James Uteg], listening to Buckethead's *Monsters and Robots*, Praxis' *Praxis Live*, Elliot Sharp's *Tectonics*, or Reid/Sharp/Torn's *Guitar Oblique*, reading online news and articles.

I came across *Why the Future Doesn't Need Us* by Bill Joy (Wired Magazine), which had a subtitle which summarized the message:

Our most powerful 21st-century technologies - robotics, genetic engineering, and nanotech - are threatening to make humans an endangered species. Joy, Chief Scientist for Sun Microsystems, had written the technological version of "There are millions of werewolves and vampires in the hills, and they are coming into the village tonight! Grandma is already a vampire! The van won't start!". It certainly got my attention.

For six years I had been out of college -an incomplete major in history, minor in political science- and no significant desire to finish it. Within a month of reading the Bill Joy article I was enrolled at Evergreen State College, pursuing a greater grasp of science and technology.

To say I was scared into going to college by Joy's luddite pessimism is not exactly correct. In 1999 I had read Ray Kurzweil's *The Age of Spiritual Machines: When Computers Exceed Human Intelligence*. Pretty much on the same topic as Joy's Why the Future Doesn't Need Us, but with exactly the opposite conclusion: we are going to alter ourselves fundamentally, and be stronger and better for it, those who don't embrace this change will be in jeopardize their survival. I originally liked the Spiritual Machines thesis, but as of 2010 have become distracted or ambivalent due to a global economic depression, and would only underperform as a husband and father if I pined for something so far off, unaffordable and self-centric.

A civil war was brewing, between two opposite conclusions regarding radical technological change. One side believing radical new technologies threaten humans with extinction, the other believing radical new technologies will help humans overcome limitations and flourish like never before. I needed an education to navigate this civil war, and also navigate if the future becomes anything like either extreme prediction.

When there is a civil war, it's hard to avoid it. I wrongly assumed I could retire to an institution, such as a monastery or university, and have several years disengaged from the war, while empowering with objective tools to aid my survival once I left. Instead, I enrolled in a place that pumped out soldiers for one side of the war.

Being a soldier indoctrination center wasn't all Evergreen State College's fault. Sure, it opened in 1967, and a construct of the dreaded New Left of that era. Regardless of the institution's origin story, the faculty and courses at the school were awesome, I learned to write both personal journals and computer code, ask good questions, and came out knowing more than when I went in. The soldier indoctrination center was a shadow institution, existing in student's dorm rooms, apartments, and out on the streets of Olympia.

The soldier indoctrination center was informal, distributed, and improvised -the very essence of 21st century successful social projects, whether they be terrorist groups or utterly peaceful communities.

While I was enrolled at the school, an Evergreen student left his classes, and Olympia, drove to Redding California, walked up to a police officer pumping gas at a convenience stop and shot him in the head. He was later arrested at a hotel on the east coast. Along with that story there's the Earth Liberation Front cell, composed of friends who met at Evergreen, who torched a UW Seattle horticulture laboratory. A few of them were caught, tried and sentenced to prison.

Leftist colleges are not the only one's prone to pumping out terroristic soldiers. While working on this chapter, on May 20, 2010, in West Memphis Arkansas, Sgt. Brandon Paudert was conducting a routine traffic stop with fellow officer Bill Evans when both were fatally shot by two individuals wielding AK-47s: 16-year-old Joseph Kane and his father, Jerry. There was a shoot-out 90 minutes later at a Wal-Mart parking lot, in which the Kanes were killed and several officers wounded.

The father and son who shot the police officers were prominent activists in the Sovereign Citizen movement, these are groups that do not recognize any form of government authority, including police forces. The father, Jerry A. Kane, wrote articles and toured the country as a preacher accusing the Obama administration of extreme leftist radicalism. They were doing their Lord's work, and driving one of their Lord's vehicles, when the police interrupted their sovereignty with a traffic citation. The van driven by the Kanes was registered to the House of God's Prayer -143 West Main Street in New Vienna. Clinton County, Ohio, a church with Aryan Nation ties.

After the shooting, local Arkansas academics in criminology were interviewed regarding the Sovereign Citizen movement, and opined that the internet is the main aid in connecting people within the movement, and also makes it difficult to tell how many members are in Arkansas.

Evidence of the internet acting as a connector and sustainer of a paranoid and racially prejudiced movement can be seen in this quote posted on a website:

> "*Where is the proof that the two vans, and the two sets of guys, are the same? Where are the videos from the cop cars, the Wal-Mart security cams, the police audio tapes, the 911 and police dispatchers? Are two cop-killer Hispanic guys still on the loose with AK47s? Will the cops try to find them, or will they just try the two dead white guys, because they can't mount a defense from the grave?*"
>
> -Tex (www.memphisflyer.com)

Reaching back to something said earlier: "*Our most powerful 21st century technologies – robots, genetic engineering and nanotech- are threatening to make humans an endangered species*" –subtitle of the Bill Joy article *Why the Future Doesn't Need Us* in Wired Magazine. The gist is big, powerful technologies such as these can slip around any defense mankind creates, and kill us. A more condensed gist: mankind makes device, device kills mankind. Now let me whip out a weapon way more powerful and more likely to kill than robotics, genetic engineering and nanotech.

Writing.

With missiles and bullets we can send something hurling through space very fast and it eventually hits and destroys a target. With radio waves we can send data or voice over great distances, in some cases a command of destruction. But writing is so very much more capable of travel. Time travel. A command can be recorded onto media (e.g. papyrus, paper, stone, concrete, or metal), buried for years, unearthed, and then read. If it is a command to destroy, bam! 5,000 year old command kills local area man.

You can try burning all books. Some will survive, and they will be back at your door, commanding a Jehovah's Witness to save you, or your descendants 5,000 years from now.

The brain is one media in which to store information. Copying is done by storytelling. Campfires are an example of data centers that many brains gather around, to do massive amounts of copying. The copying is free and non-rivalrous*, especially if done while doing other work. Stories of Greek gods got their start with this kind of media storage and transfer, for at least a thousand years before being recorded by Homer and Plato on an alternative media: papyrus.

[* In economics, a public good is a good that is non-rivalrous and non-excludable. Non-rivalry means consumption of the good by one individual does not reduce availability of the good for consumption by others; and non-excludability means no one can be effectively excluded from using the good.]

All things are not equal. Storage data on non-brain media is very different from storing on brain media. During copying, brains do something unique: when the story is retrieved, it is sent across a lot of internal brain processes, and while traveling across these electrical stages the story changes -sometimes a little, sometimes a lot.

Storing on media other than the brain diminishes deviance and corruption of the story, at least at the hardware level. Of course, there's still a lot of deviance humans can enlist at the interpretive level, such as reading "Caesar is greater than all" and using one's academic authority combined with a little bit of attitude to report to anyone listening the message actually says "Caesar is trying to compensate for a declining empire".

On a flight from Los Angeles to Auckland New Zealand in August 1995 I read Umberto Eco's *A Theory of Semiotics* -one of my all-time favorite books. Eco claims that interpretation operates on a ratio of two opposites: *interpretive license* and *historical accuracy*. To illustrate this, take the story of Jesus in the New Testament. A 12-year-old Caucasian female reads the Biblical account, in 1986, while she lives in Oklahoma. Her goal is to find a story that is deeply religious and transforming, she can relate to, and she can incorporate into her lifestyle. With the account of Jesus, if she adheres totally to historical accuracy she has to emphasize it's a Jewish story, set in the Fertile Crescent, 2,000 years ago, and the main character is a male. It is very hard, or impossible, to replicate the life-style of a religious figure from 2,000 years ago if you are a 12 year old girl in 1980's Oklahoma. Interpretive license allows for vastly more wiggle room, and maybe the 12-year-old girl can somehow translate the story of Jesus into life-style choices she can actually perform. She chooses to go with 20 percent historical accuracy and 80 percent interpretive license.

It's healthy to get a mix of interpretive license and historical accuracy, but maybe there is more of a career in overworking one and omitting the other. Since the 1970's Postmodernists gained academic tenure and sold books abusing interpretive license and religious fundamentalists (especially Protestants in the USA and Muslims in the Middle East) have gotten converts via claims to their faith's adherence to historical accuracy in regards to a particular religious text.

The fundamentalists return us to writing as time travel for commands. Fundamentalists are the key ingredients for making old religious texts come to life and commit political acts on contemporary streets. Fundamentalists make for as scary of a scenario as any of Bill Joy's fears.

While writing creates havoc, it is a better fate than the entropic trap called illiteracy. Recording our thoughts on an external media allows for a saving up of thoughts, and a scaling up of thoughts. A civilized, literate man may not contain complexity or dimensions greater than an uncivilized, illiterate man. Advantage comes when the literate individual utilizes something with dimensional scale larger than occurs in nature: civilization stored on media other than the brain, encoded in text and numbers. When this information is retrieved, used with skill and calculation, the human is empowered to a degree that outperforms nature, and often leads to owning nature.

Speaking of ownership, there may be no rights to living space without literate record. Without writing, people's relation to a place to reside is tentatively based on the whims of war and sectarian alliance. Writing, employed within civic institutions of justice, provides an objective claim to living space -only then can a human lucidly assume a state of peace regarding what they call home or homeland.

The only placid context resides in the stormy relationship called civilization, personified by Athena.

The mutating force of Athena Techne is so impressively complex she generates her own threats, which she then uses as an evolutionary pressure to improve to a more complex stage. Athena Techne is an unstoppable force, much like 21st century technologies feared by many, and it is realistic to hope her role, much like a virus, will continue to live indefinitely within her host we could call the natural universe.

You can try burning this book, and this hope. Athena Techne is going to public domain after my passing. Consequently, this hope will easily live on, routing around any petty bonfire or policy committee.

Athena Techne will be back at your door, enlisting the demiurge to save civilization from the vices of your age.

Bibliography

Ahl,Valerie and Allen, .T.F.H. **Hierarchy Theory -A Vision, Vocabulary, and Epistemology** (pp. 169-171). Columbia University Press 1996.

Adorno, Theodor W. and Hullot-Kentor, Robert. **Aesthetic Theory**. University of Minnesota Press, 1998

Atwill Janet. **Rhetoric reclaimed: Aristotle and the liberal arts tradition**. Cornell University Press. February 1998

Dyson, Freeman. **Interview by Monte Davis**. 1978 (reused in **Athena Techne** with rights granted via personal email with Freeman Dyson.)

Joy, Bill. **Why the Future Doesn't Need Us**. Wired Issue 8.04 April 2000.

Kurzweil, Ray. **The Age of Spiritual Machines: When Computers Exceed Human Intelligence**. Viking Adult 1999.

Lyotard, Jean-Francois. **The Lyotard Reader**. Blackwell Publishers, 1989.

Robb, John. **The Systempunkt**
Retrieved from
http://globalguerrillas.typepad.com/globalguerrillas/2004/12/the_systempunkt.html blog entry December 19, 2004.
(term used in **Athena Techne** with rights granted via personal email with John Robb.)

Index

Made in the USA
Charleston, SC
10 February 2011